TRANSPORTATION
Activity Book

ALAIN GRÉE

Button
BOOKS

Transportation traffic

Look carefully at this picture. How many different vehicles can you see?
Which one is the fastest? Which vehicle uses wind power to move around?
Add some stickers if you like.

Scooter pairs

Find the matching scooters and color them in the same.

Blast off! Solve the math problems to find out
which rocket will be the first to launch. The rocket with
the highest number is the one that will go first.

Racecar fun

Trace around the two blue cars onto a piece of card stock and then color them in. Stick to each side of a horizontal cardboard tube to create your own racecar. You can make a few in different colors to race with your friends.

Different vehicles

Unscramble the names of these different vehicles and write your answers in the boxes underneath. Then draw a picture of your favorite vehicle and color it in.

ubs

domep

broomekit

urkct

celciby

rolltey

[ ]

prosst arc

[ ]

blace rac

[ ]

artin

[ ]

Funny transportation

Q: Where do astronauts keep their sandwiches?
A: In a launch box.

Q: Which vegetable would you never want on your boat?
A: A leek.

Q: What do you call a train that sneezes?
A: A choo-achoo train.

Odd one out

Which car is the odd one out?

True or false?

There are 12 people on the bus.

On the roof there are 7 pink birds.

The man on the bicycle has a red feather in his hat.

Row the boat

Color in both of these pictures using completely different colors for each one.

Boat race

Choose words from the sticker pages to finish this watery adventure.

One sunny day a [____] and a [____] had a race.

The speedboat said, "I will win because I am much [____] and

more [____] than you." So the two boats set off and the speedboat

was really [____]. But she went so quickly she ran out of [____]

and stopped suddenly. The sailing boat, who just used the [____] to fill

her sails, soon [____] the speedboat and won the race!

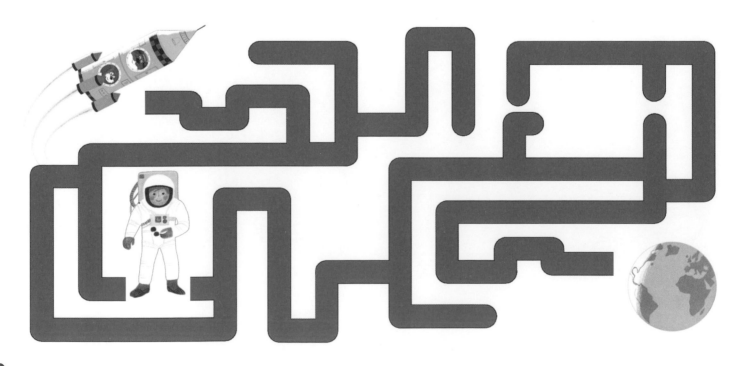

Lost in space

Can you help the spaceship find its way home to Earth?
Don't forget to collect the astronaut on your way!

Up in the air

Can you find these air and space transportation-related words in the puzzle?

```
p  i  l  o  t  m  w  a  z  m  o  c
m  t  z  x  h  o  p  s  s  t  q  r
r  b  n  r  e  t  a  t  s  m  u  b
o  j  m  o  l  o  r  r  t  a  g  a
c  n  w  c  i  r  a  o  o  p  l  l
k  g  f  k  c  b  c  n  a  h  i  l
e  m  v  e  o  i  h  a  i  w  d  o
t  o  u  t  p  k  u  u  n  o  e  o
s  a  t  k  t  e  t  t  n  s  r  n
p  l  a  n  e  l  e  u  t  i  l  d
r  p  k  o  r  m  s  p  a  c  e  s
m  o  o  n  b  u  g  g  y  d  h  b
```

helicopter

balloon

plane

rocket

space

moon buggy

astronaut

pilot

glider

parachute

Sailboat pairs

Find the matching pairs. Which is the odd one out?

Disappearing act

This plane is disappearing into the clouds. Color in the side of the plane so that it matches the other side.

Odd ones out

Two of these boats are the same. Can you spot which boats are different?

Ready for takeoff

Which truck is fueling the plane? Follow the colored lines to find out.

Find the sacks

How many sacks of flour can you see in this picture? Don't forget to look in the freight car, too.

Onto the ferry

Put these pictures in order to load the car onto the ferry. Write numbers in the circles—number 1 has been done for you.

Dotty helicopter

Join the dots to complete this helicopter, then color it in.

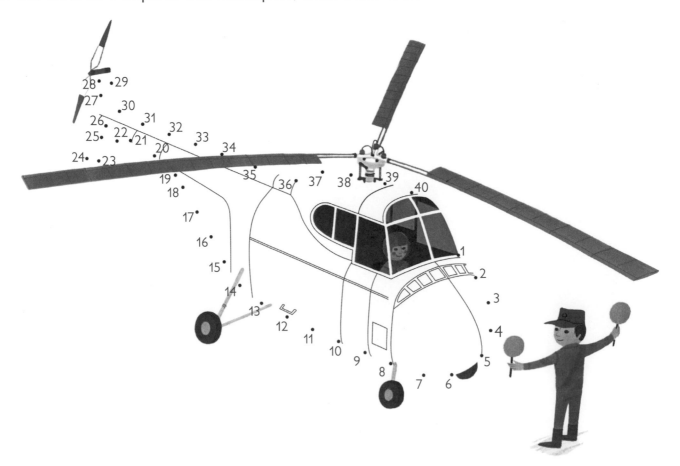

Spot the difference

Can you spot five differences between these two pictures?

Moon buggy run

Help the space buggy get across the moon without hitting any craters.

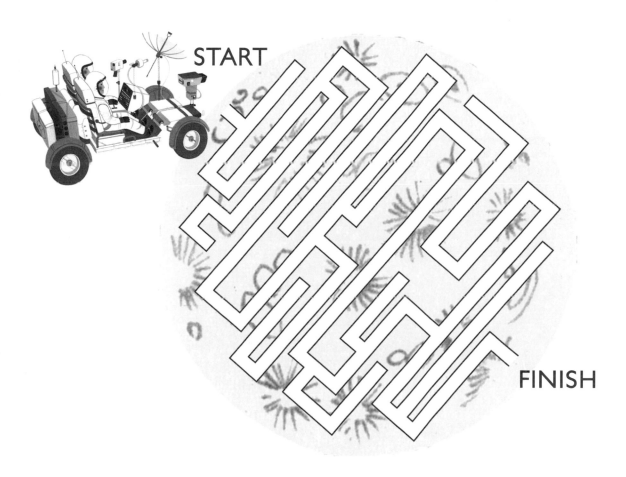

START

FINISH

Gone fishing

How many fish can you spot on this boat? Decorate the page with some stickers from the sticker pages, too.

Odd one out

Can you spot which is the odd one out?

Cycle race

Will the cyclist or the motorcycle rider make it to the finish?
Follow the trails to find out.

FINISH

Connect the pictures

Choose words from the box and write the correct one underneath each picture. Then can you match each picture in the box on the left with one in the box on the right? For example, the boat goes with the anchor.

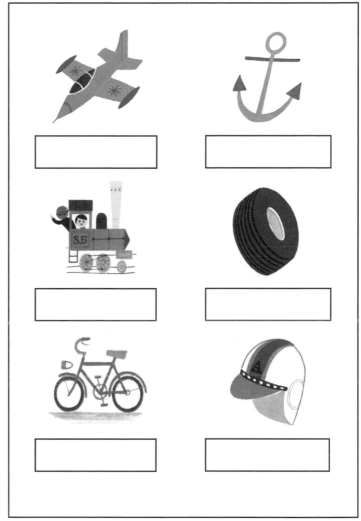

train	anchor
bicycle	motorbike
track	helmet
car	parachute
wheel	airplane
boat	cyclist

Missing pieces

Help the conductor to find the missing train cars. Write the number of each missing piece in the spaces with the question marks. How many cars and trucks can you see?

Catching the bus

Help Polly find her way to the bus stop.

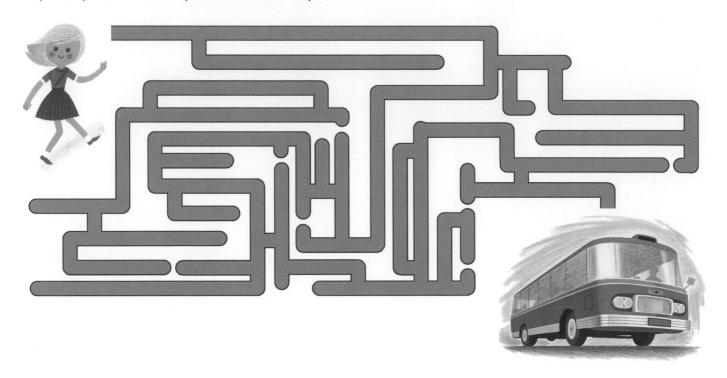

Find the pairs

Can you find the four matching trains? Draw a line between them to match them up.

Dinghy dot to dot

Join the dots to complete this picture, then color it in.
You can add some stickers if you like, too.

Ready, set, go!

Which racecar will reach the finish? Follow the tangled lines to find out.

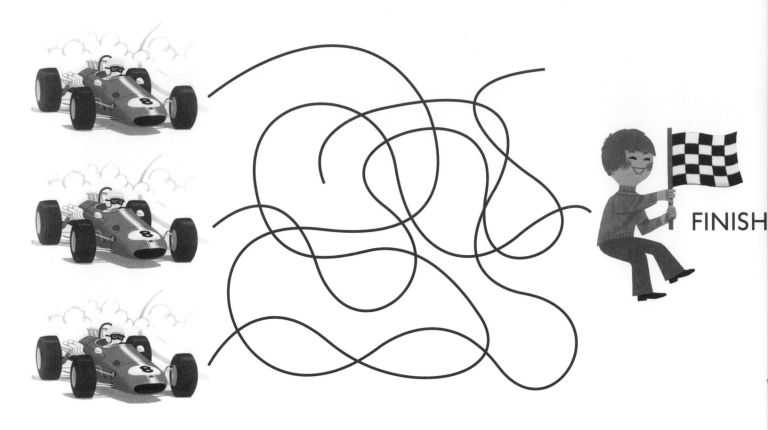

FINISH

Odd one out

Which of these train conductors is the odd one out?

Sunny day out

Polly, Jack, and Ben are going out for a picnic. Help them find their way to the shady picnic spot. Remember to pick up bread on the way, and try not to break down!

Wheel deal

Count how many wheels you can see on each of these engines.
Which engine has the most wheels?

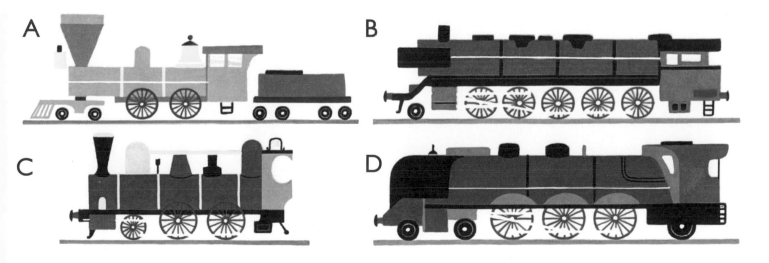

A

B

C

D

Raft rift

Can you spot five differences between these two rafting scenes?

Twin sets

Can you find the three matching pairs of bicycles? Draw lines between them to match them up.

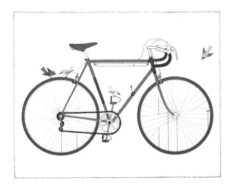  

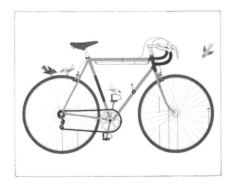 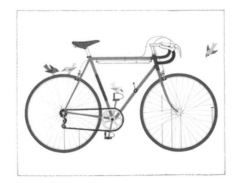 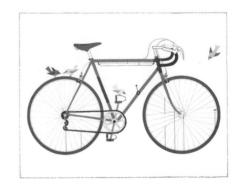

Parachute math

Do the math problems to find out which parachute will land first—it's the one with the highest number. Then unscramble the letters to find out which food item is in the box.

9 + 6 =

6 + 12 =

20 - 3 =

sanbana

Ship shape

Can you work out which silhouette matches the ship?

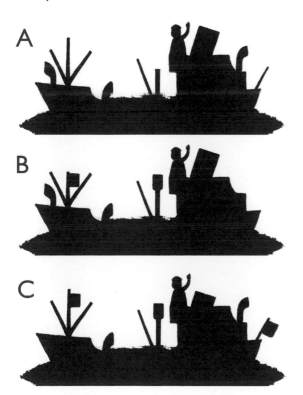

A

B

C

D

E

Highway codes

Can you match each road sign with its description?

slippery road

no passing

no pedestrians

maximum speed

no bicycles

road work

Midnight express

How many windows are there on the train? How many columns can you see on the viaduct?

Odd one out

Which rower is the odd one out?

Runaway cable car

The cable car is running away down the hill.
Draw around the outline, then color it in.

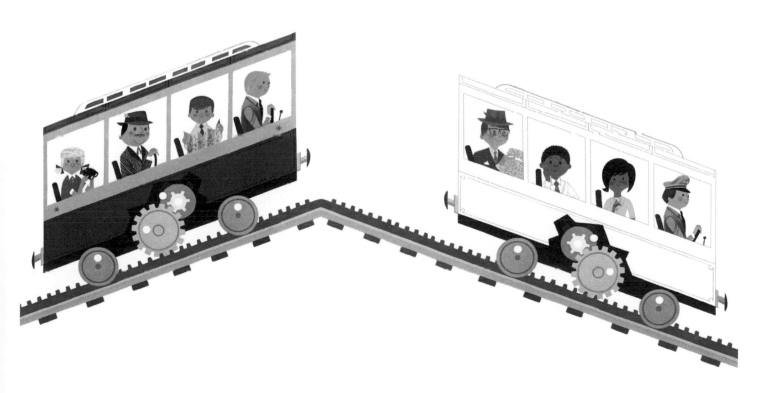

Rocket launch

Put these pictures in order to show the different stages of a rocket launch.
Write numbers in the circles—numbers 1, 3, and 8 have been done for you.

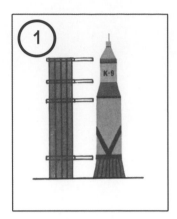

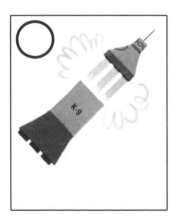

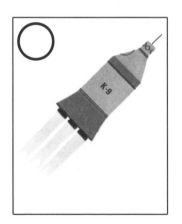

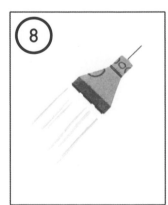

Sail away

Which dinghy is the fastest? Do the math problems to find out. The highest number is the quickest dinghy.

$5+3-4=$ ◯

$1+5+7=$ ◯

$6+2-1=$ ◯

Map reading

Start at Green Park station. Go two stops to the right on the red line, then two stops to the left on the green line. Change to the yellow line and go one stop to the right. Where are you?

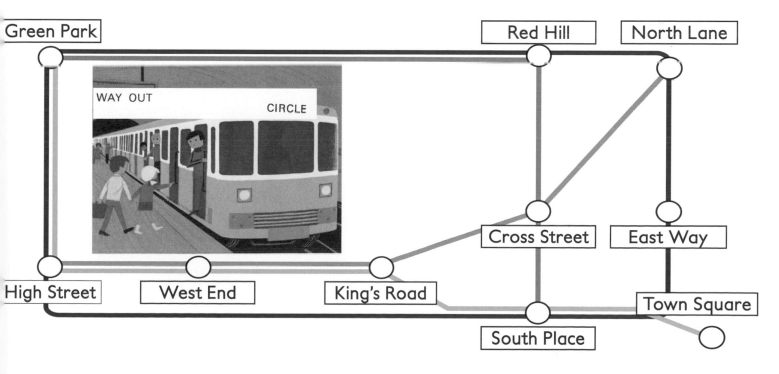

Going on a journey

Find the stickers that match the 20 small pictures, and group them with the right method of transportation: air, sea, road, and rail.

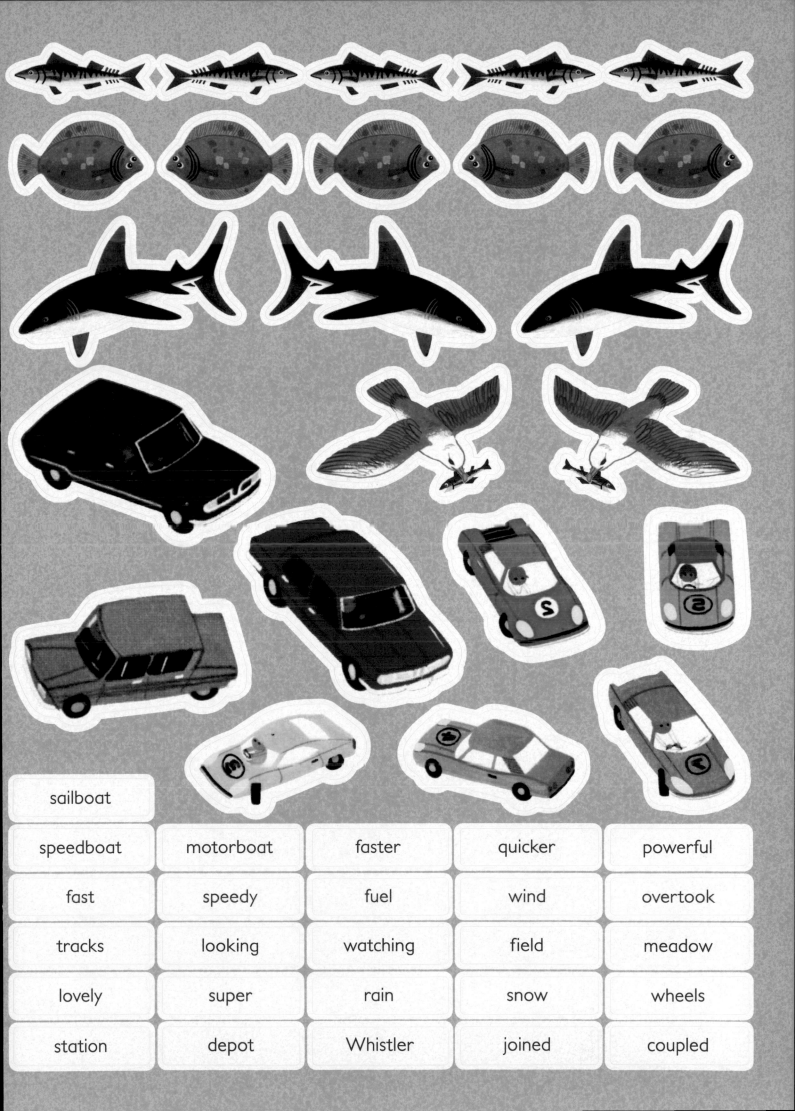

sailboat

speedboat | motorboat | faster | quicker | powerful
fast | speedy | fuel | wind | overtook
tracks | looking | watching | field | meadow
lovely | super | rain | snow | wheels
station | depot | Whistler | joined | coupled

STEF

33

Traveling by train

Unscramble the letters to work out which countries these trains come from and write the countries underneath. Look at the list for some help.

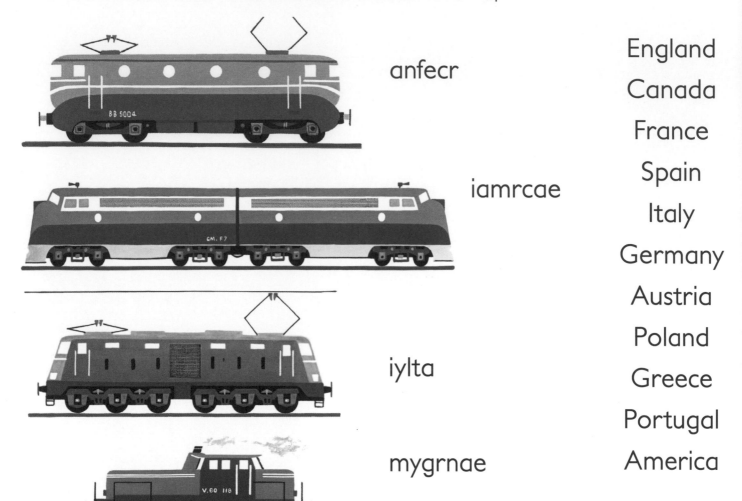

anfecr

iamrcae

iylta

mygrnae

England
Canada
France
Spain
Italy
Germany
Austria
Poland
Greece
Portugal
America

Speedboat fun

Draw the other half of this picture, then color it in.

Spot the difference

Can you spot five differences between these two pictures?

Find the boat

Can you find these different types of boat hidden in the puzzle?

g s p e e d b o a t e s
a i b g h j h l a c q u
l b a r g n e f a m u b
l j r b b d f e r r y m
e n g c a i l m c a h a
o k e r h n s u a c q r
n k a y a k l n n h r i
e o u t t h e o o t e n
y a c h t y n m e s v e
z n d e e p s u t n i d
r o w b o a t o e c r s
m o t u g b o a t d d b

tugboat
galleon
yacht
canoe
ferry
barge
speedboat
rowboat
kayak
submarine

Lunch stop

Help these travelers find the way to the bakery to get some bread for their lunch.

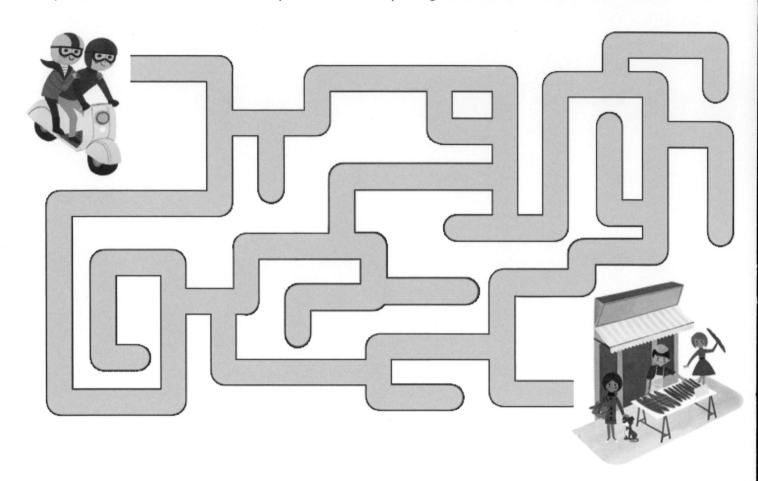

The runaway train

Choose words from the sticker pages to finish this train adventure.

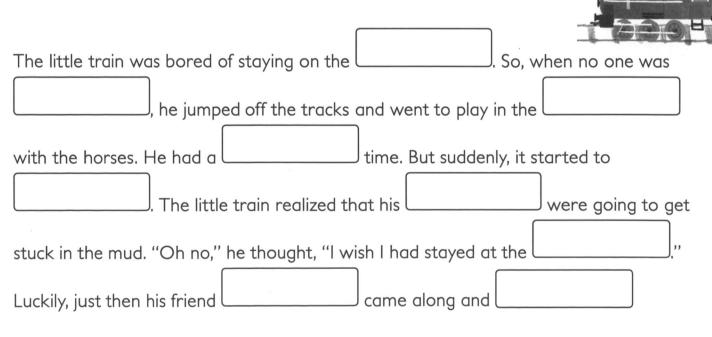

The little train was bored of staying on the [_____]. So, when no one was

[_____], he jumped off the tracks and went to play in the [_____]

with the horses. He had a [_____] time. But suddenly, it started to

[_____]. The little train realized that his [_____] were going to get

stuck in the mud. "Oh no," he thought, "I wish I had stayed at the [_____]."

Luckily, just then his friend [_____] came along and [_____]

them together. "Thank you so much," said the little train. "I'll never run away again!"

Land ahoy!

Color in this picture, then draw an island in the distance.
Add some stickers of seagulls and fish, too.

Make a model train car

Make your own train car by following these four steps.
Ask a grown-up for help.

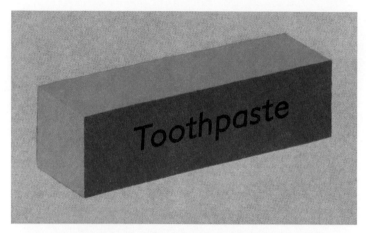

1. Take an empty toothpaste box.

You will need:
1 toothpaste box
1 sheet of 8½ x 11-inch paper
scissors, hobby knife, and glue
pencils, ruler, and crayons
2 corks and 12 thumbtacks

2. Cut a piece of paper big enough to wrap around three long sides of the box. Copy this pattern onto it.

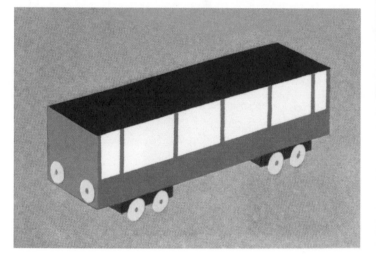

4. Wrap the paper around the box and glue the pieces of cork underneath. Stick two more thumbtacks into the back to complete the train car.

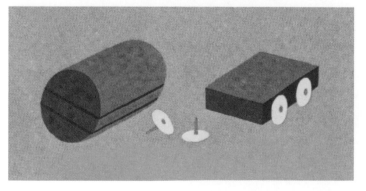

3. Cut two pieces of cork as shown here. Pin four thumbtacks to each piece of cork.

Spot the difference

Spot five differences between these two pictures.

Off to work

This man is late for work! Help him get to the train station on time.

Road sticker fun

Add some stickers of cars and road signs to this picture.

Boats with oars and paddles

What are the different kinds of water transportation here? Choose the right words from the list and write the word by each one. Then draw your own boat next to the boy and color it in.

raft

kayak

steamboat

motorboat

dinghy

submarine

longboat

canoe

Motor math

Work out the math problems on these cars to find out which one goes the fastest—it's the car with the highest number.

7 + 6 =

11 - 3 =

3 + 9 =

7 + 5 =

Dotty airplane

Join the dots to find the airplane and then color it in.

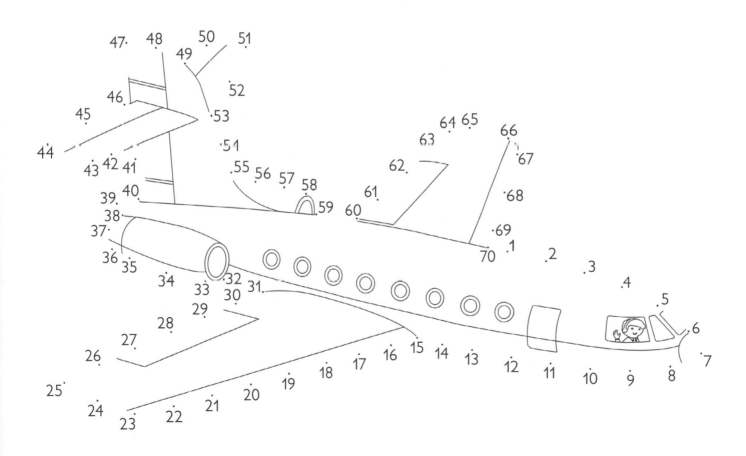

Spot the difference

Spot five differences between these two pictures.

 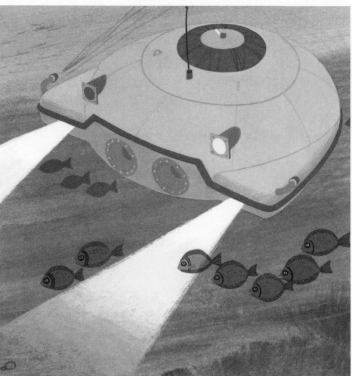

Racecar maze

Can you help this racecar driver get to his car before the race starts?

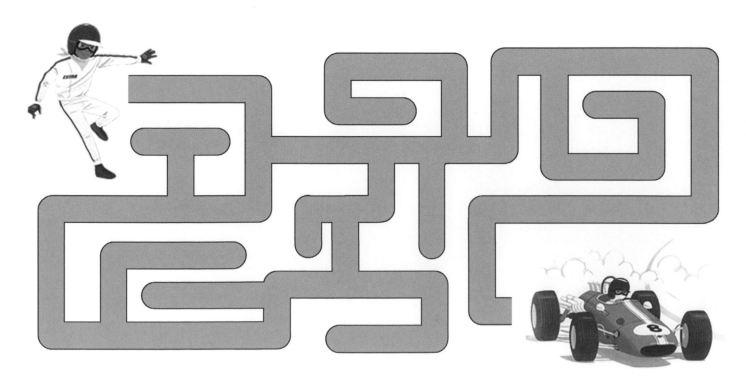

Parachute fun

How many blue parachutes can you spot in the picture?

How many parachutes are there altogether?

True or false: there are three parachutes attached to a jeep.

All aboard the bus

Add some passengers and a driver to this bus, then color in the picture.

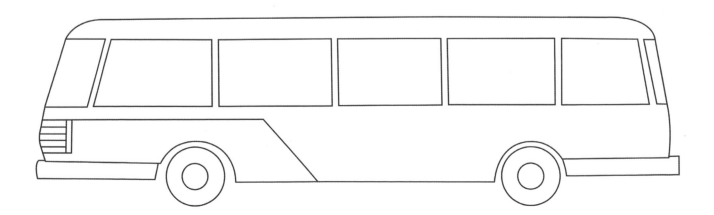

Trolley lines

Help Polly travel from trolley stop A to meet Jack at trolley stop L. Draw a line along the route with the fewest stops. How many times does she need to change to a different colored line?

Odd one out

Which one of these compasses is the odd one out?

Sailboat coloring

Color in this ancient Egyptian boat, then draw some pyramids and camels in the background. You can add some stickers, too.

All muddled up

Unscramble the words of these objects in the picture. Then color in the viaduct.

geenin

caitvud

itarn

nuntle

debirg

ganow

scratk

Ocean liner dot to dot

Join the dots to complete the ocean liner, then color it in.

Silly jokes

Q: Why can't a bicycle stand up for itself?
A: Because it is two-tired.

Q: What do you call a flying policeman?
A: A helicopper.

Q: Which item of clothing does
a train travel over?
A: Railroad ties.

Filling up

Three lines are connected to the tanker, but only one is connected to the fuel tank. Can you work out which one it is?

Trailer tally

How many barrels are there on the trailers? How many birds can you see?

Heavy weights

Do the math problems to find out which airship will reach the ground first.
The airship with the highest number is the one that will land first.

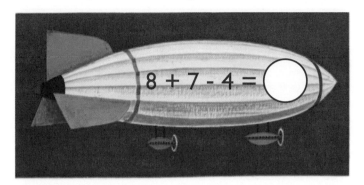

$8 + 7 - 4 =$ ◯

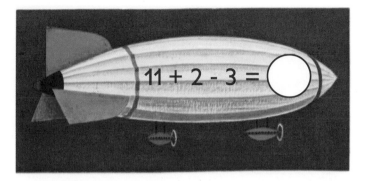

$11 + 2 - 3 =$ ◯

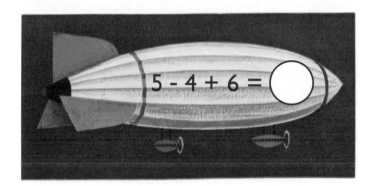

$5 - 4 + 6 =$ ◯

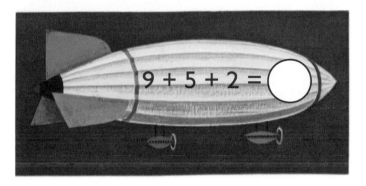

$9 + 5 + 2 =$ ◯

Steaming ahead

How many flags and pennants are there on this paddle steamer?
Count the people, too.
How many windows are there?
Can you tell which country it's from? (Clue: look at the flag on the right.)

C. JAMES

Winter race

Find the racecar stickers and add them to this page.

How many people are watching the race?

Going underground

How many people can you see in this busy subway station?
How many of them are wearing glasses?
Can you find the dog in the picture?

Ocean vessels

Put these boats in order of size by writing numbers in the circles, from 1 for the smallest to 9 for the biggest. Numbers 1 and 9 have been done for you.

 (1)

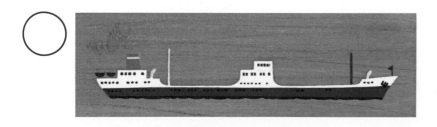

(9)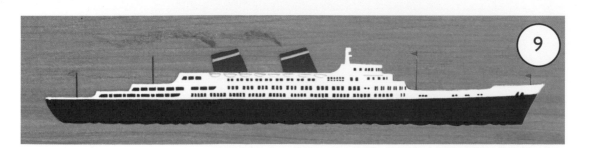

Odd one out

Which rocket is the odd one out?

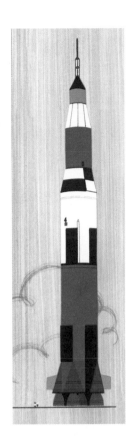

Travel search

Can you find these words hidden in the puzzle?

r	o	a	d	c	s	d	r	i	m	o	t
a	t	r	g	s	c	r	w	a	o	q	a
r	b	n	a	g	o	i	f	s	t	g	x
t	j	m	o	n	o	v	j	e	o	n	i
m	n	w	c	s	t	e	t	r	r	i	k
e	n	g	i	n	e	r	u	t	b	l	s
t	m	v	e	u	r	e	o	r	i	i	w
e	o	u	b	c	h	l	c	u	k	a	h
y	o	m	u	t	y	l	m	c	e	s	i
z	n	l	s	d	p	e	v	k	e	l	d
b	i	c	y	c	l	e	m	a	e	t	s
h	c	a	r	s	v	a	n	h	r	h	b

road

taxi

bicycle

car

van

motorbike

bus

driver

engine

truck

scooter

Transportation traffic (page 2)

There are 9 different vehicles:
airplane, ocean liner, helicopter, fishing
boat, sailboat, train, moped, truck, car.
The airplane is the fastest.
The sailboat uses wind power.

Odd one out (page 8)

True or false (page 9)

True: there are 12 people on the bus.
True: there are 7 pink birds on the roof.
False: the man on the bicycle has a yellow
feather in his hat.

Scooter pairs (page 4)

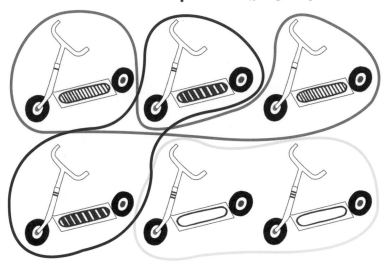

Lost in space (page 10)

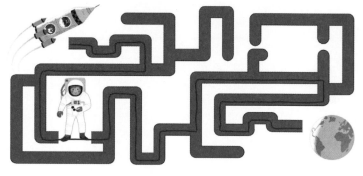

Blast off! (page 4)

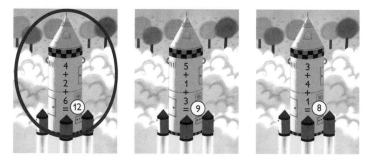

4 + 2 + 6 = 12

5 + 1 + 3 = 9

3 + 4 + 1 = 8

Up in the air (page 11)

p	i	l	o	t	m	w	a	z	m	o	c
m	t	z	x	h	o	p	s	s	t	q	r
r	b	n	r	e	t	a	t	s	m	u	b
o	j	m	o	l	o	r	r	t	a	g	a
c	n	w	c	i	r	a	o	o	p	l	l
k	g	f	k	c	b	c	n	a	h	i	l
e	m	v	e	o	i	h	a	i	w	d	o
t	o	u	t	p	k	u	u	n	o	e	o
s	a	t	k	t	e	t	t	n	s	r	n
p	l	a	n	e	l	e	u	t	i	l	d
r	p	k	o	r	m	s	p	a	c	e	s
m	o	o	n	b	u	g	g	y	d	h	b

Different vehicles (page 6)

domep = moped   rolltey = trolley

celciby = bicycle   blace rac =

ubs = bus   cable car

broomekit =   prosst arc =

motorbike   sports car

urkct = truck   artin = train

Sailboat pairs (page 11)

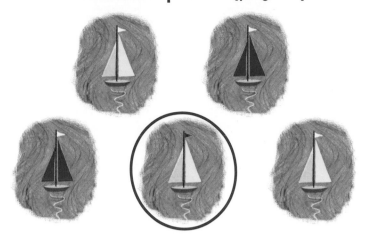

Onto the ferry (page 14)

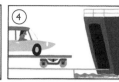

Odd ones out (page 12)

Spot the difference (page 15)

Moon buggy run (page 15)

Ready for takeoff (page 13)

Gone fishing (page 16)

There are 19 fish.

Find the sacks (page 13)

There are 9 sacks of flour.

Odd one out (page 18)

Cycle race (page 18)

FINISH

Catching the bus (page 22)

Connect the pictures (page 19)

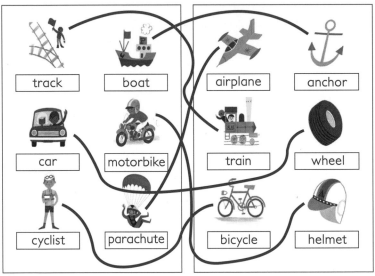

track | boat | airplane | anchor
car | motorbike | train | wheel
cyclist | parachute | bicycle | helmet

Find the pairs (page 22)

Ready, set, go! (page 24)

FINISH

Missing pieces (page 20)

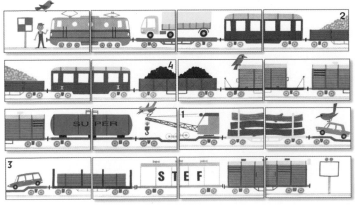

There are 2 cars.
There is 1 truck.

Odd one out (page 24)

Sunny day out (page 25)

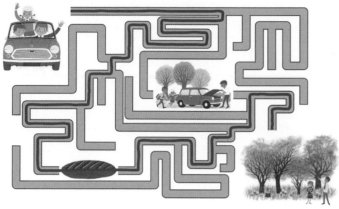

Wheel deal (page 25)

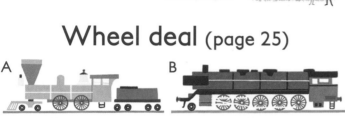

 8 wheels   6 wheels

 3 wheels   6 wheels

Train A has the most wheels.

Raft rift (page 26)

Twin sets (page 26)

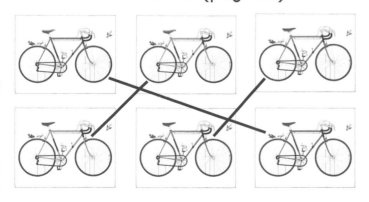

Parachute math (page 27)

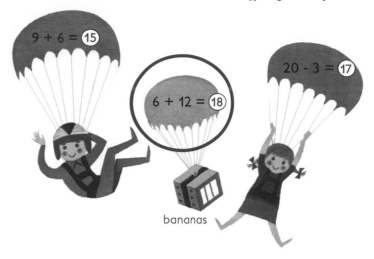

9 + 6 = 15

6 + 12 = 18

20 - 3 = 17

bananas

Ship shape (page 27)

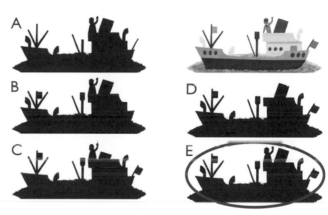

Highway codes (page 28)

 no passing   maximum speed   road work

 slippery road   no pedestrians   no bicycles

Midnight express (page 28)

There are 26 windows on the train.

The viaduct has 12 columns.

Answers

Odd one out (page 29)

Rocket launch (page 30)

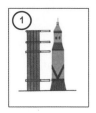

Sail away (page 31)

Map reading (page 31)

You are at South Place.

Going on a journey (page 32)

Traveling by train (page 34)

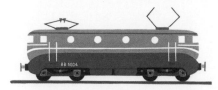 France

 America

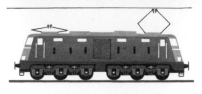 Italy

 Germany

Spot the difference (page 35)

Find the boat (page 35)

g	s	p	e	e	d	b	o	a	t	e	s
g	i	b	g	h	j	h	l	a	c	q	u
a	b	a	r	g	n	e	f	a	m	u	b
l	j	r	b	b	d	f	e	r	r	y	m
l	n	g	c	a	i	l	m	c	a	h	a
e	k	e	r	h	n	s	u	a	c	q	r
o	k	a	y	a	k	l	n	n	h	r	i
n	e	o	u	t	t	h	e	o	o	t	n
y	a	c	h	t	y	n	m	e	s	v	e
z	n	d	e	e	p	s	u	t	n	i	d
r	o	w	b	o	a	t	o	e	c	r	s
m	o	t	u	g	b	o	a	t	d	d	b

60

Lunch stop (page 36)

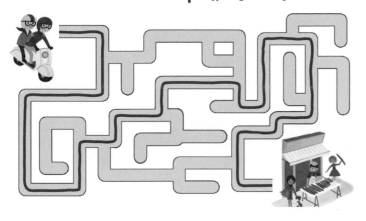

Spot the difference (page 39)

Off to work (page 39)

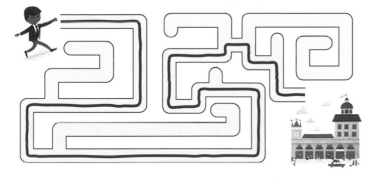

Boats with oars and paddles
(page 42)

canoe

kayak

longboat

dinghy

Motor math (page 43)

7 + 6 = 13

11 - 3 = 8

3 + 9 = 12

7 + 5 = 12

Spot the difference (page 44)

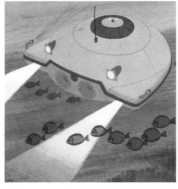
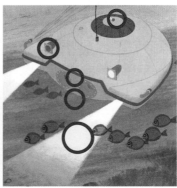

Racecar maze (page 44)

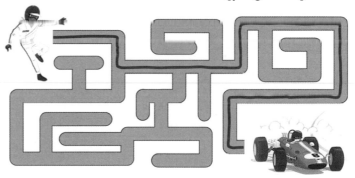

Parachute fun (page 45)

There are 3 blue parachutes.

There are 17 parachutes altogether.

True: there are 3 parachutes attached

to a jeep.

Trolley lines (page 46)

Polly needs to change 3 times onto a different colored line.

Odd one out (page 46)

All muddled up (page 48)

geenin = engine   caitvud = viaduct
itarn = train   nuntle = tunnel
debirg = bridge   ganow = wagon
scratk = tracks

Filling up (page 50)

Trailer tally (page 51)

There are 7 barrels and 6 birds in the picture.

Heavy weights (page 51)

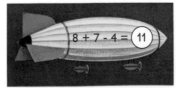

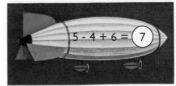

8 + 7 - 4 = 11

11 + 2 - 3 = 10

5 - 4 + 6 = 7

9 + 5 + 2 = 16

Steaming ahead (page 51)

There are 4 flags and pennants.
There are 18 people.
There are 43 windows.
The paddle steamer is from the USA.

Winter race (page 52)
31 people are watching the race.

Ocean vessels (page 54)

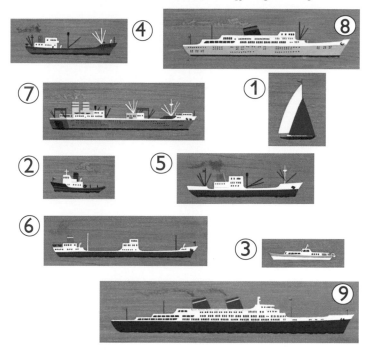

Odd one out (page 55)

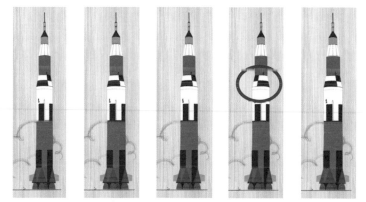

Going underground (page 53)

29 people are in the picture.
3 people are wearing glasses.

Travel search (page 55)

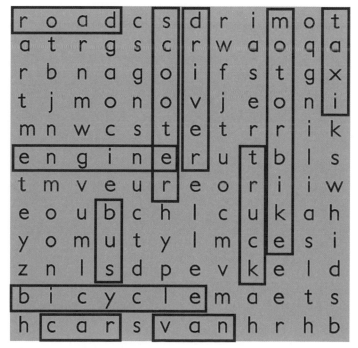

First published 2019 by Button Books, an imprint of Guild of Master Craftsman Publications Ltd, Castle Place, 166 High Street, Lewes, East Sussex BN7 1XU, UK. Text © GMC Publications Ltd, 2019. Copyright in the Work © GMC Publications Ltd, 2019. Illustrations © 2019 A.G. & RicoBel. ISBN 978 1 78708 023 2. Distributed by Publishers Group West in the United States. All rights reserved. The right of Alain Grée to be identified as the illustrator of this work has been asserted in accordance with the Copyright, Designs, and Patents Act 1988, sections 77 and 78. No part of this publication may be reproduced, stored in a retrieval system, or transmitted in any form, or by any means without the prior permission of the publisher and copyright owner. While every effort has been made to obtain permission from the copyright holders for all material used in this book, the publishers will be pleased to hear from anyone who has not been appropriately acknowledged and to make the correction in future reprints. The publishers and author can accept no legal responsibility for any consequences arising from the application of information, advice, or instructions given in this publication. A catalog record for this book is available from the British Library. Publisher: Jonathan Bailey. Production: Jim Bulley, Jo Pallett. Senior Project Editor: Sara Harper. Managing Art Editor: Gilda Pacitti. Designer: Alex Bailey. Americanizer: Betsy Hamilton. Color origination by GMC Reprographics. Printed and bound in China. Warning! Choking hazard—small parts. Not suitable for children under 3 years.